Seven Tails

Seven Tails

Lolita Lanning

Illustrated by
Susanna Dupont-Patmon
& Harlene Schwartz

Printed in the United States of America

06   05   04   03   02   1   2   3   4   5

Library of Congress Catalog Card Number: 2001096659

ISBN: 1-57736-255-1

Cover design by Gary Bozeman

Cover illustrations by Susanna Dupont Patmon and Harlene Schwartz

Illustrations on pages 11, 18, 21, 26, 37, 41, 47, 50, 59, 60, 70, 74, 77, and 81 by Susanna Dupont Patmon.

Illustrations on pages 13, 22, 32, 52, 66, and 82 by Harlene Schwartz.

Hillsboro Press
PROVIDENCE PUBLISHING CORPORATION
238 Seaboard Lane Franklin, Tennessee 37067
800-321-5692
www.providencepubcorp.com

To
my children
Larry and Mitch Abbott,
and
Bryan and Marisa Lanning.
They put magic in my past.
And
to my grandchildren,
Corwin and Annalee Abbott,
Rowan and Gwynn Lanning—
future magic.

Contents

Acknowledgments

My thanks and admiration go to Anne Lowenkopf, who publishes under the names John Major Hurdy and Marika Kriss. Whatever name she goes by, I am fortunate to call her my editor and honored to call her my friend. It is because of Anne that these essays became a book.

My heart is grateful for the friendship and support of Barnaby Conrad and his wonderful wife, Mary. What giving and caring people they are, and how I appreciate their encouragement.

I am especially beholden to Susanna Dupont Patmon for her tender and loving illustrations. Her light illuminates our book as well as my life.

Dr. George "Tad" Porter brought me together with the marvelous people at Providence House Publishers. I thank him with a full heart.

And my love and thanks go to my "in-law children:" Roxie Abbott, Jennifer Lanning, and Stan Lanning. They believed in me, and so this little book took flight.

Seven Tails

The Coming of Poi Dog

Imagine a storm of such ferocity that the palm trees bent over double and flagged at right angles to the ground. Where sand on the beach blew twenty feet into the air, and the rain made pebbles of dirt dance like hailstones. Out of such a storm, on such a night, he came into our lives.

Unable to sleep, I prowled the living room of the spacious house we had rented for the summer, sliding open some opposing windows in fear they might break. For although the storm was frightening, the air was warm. We were on the island of Oahu in Kahuku, Hawaii. Turning from one wall of windows, my eye was caught by a movement on the large lanai that wrapped around the front of the house. I slid open the screen door and switched on the light. And there stood Himself, soaking wet but with his head held high, bone-poking thin yet with such a regal air about him, he caught my heart. He was caked in the red clay Hawaiians call mud. For a breath's-held second we stared at one another, he poised to run, I ready to love.

"Well, poor fellow, you poor, poor, boy," I crooned, advancing slowly, hand outstretched to let him sniff me. He looked back over his shoulder. Yes, he did. Could there be some unfortunate beast behind him? Certainly he didn't see himself as such. Smiling, I sat down in a roomy wicker chair and I waited.

He came to me. Never taking his eyes from mine, he snuffled my hand and then rewarded me with a little aloha kiss, his warm tongue crossing my palm tentatively. The best I could do for him was a can of roast beef hash and a bowl of water. He ate slowly, but he ate it all. Yet, when I invited him into the house to sleep, he declined my offer. Perhaps he found it inappropriate to bring his mud-encrusted self into a house with white furniture. Instead, he curled up on a hemp mat just outside the glass doors, deep in the haven of our lanai; and there he spent the night.

My sleep was shattered by cries of delight from my four children when, at 6:00 A.M., two of them presented themselves bedside and announced, all twinkly eyed: "Mom, we have a dog."

The new day brought a close encounter of the necessary kind for Himself and for me. We found ourselves enclosed in a stall shower with a bottle of baby shampoo. My date. Himself was simply terrified, and he kept trying to climb the sheer tile walls of the shower. Midway through his bath it occurred to me that here I was in a sealed container with a medium-sized dog I scarcely knew and who was equipped with a full set of sharp teeth. He *could* use them on me. I knew he would not.

That first day also brought us to market in the village of Kahuku to buy such necessities as dog food (my idea) and squeaky toys, chew bones, and a ball (the children's idea). We also made inquiries as to the dog's ownership. We described him to the market owner, the postmaster, and assorted villagers.

"Oh, probably he's a poi dog," they said. "You know, just a Hawaiian poi dog. Not likely anyone will claim him. You like, you keep."

"A poi dog. And what exactly is that?"

"Oh, you know. A stray dog, a drifter, wanders the beach. Sometime the locals, they share their poi with him, and so he gets the name poi dog. Has been in Hawaii hundreds years."

Happy yaps from the lanai greeted our return to the house and our "hundreds years" poi dog bounced down the steps. A poi dog looks like the Australian dingo, or wild dog. He has a short reddish

coat, pricked ears, and a tail that curves but is carried low. He is about the size of a standard smooth-coated fox terrier and has an alert, intelligent expression. In the years since that summer of 1975 I have seen many poi dogs, both in ancient drawings and in person, and they all look exactly the same. Our poi dog looked like he'd been dug up after a hundred years, but if he was oblivious to his moth-eaten coat, why then, so were we.

By the second day Himself had taken on the job of guard dog, bounding down the driveway at any approaching car, barking loudly and prepared to defend us against all manner of evildoers. It would also seem that he would not be moving on. He was soaking up love like a little canine sponge, devouring two well-balanced meals a day, getting brushed hourly, and sleeping undisturbed on his hemp mat.

And so he must have a name. The children came up with Poochie. Right. Mr. Poochie maybe or King Poochie in keeping with his dignity. But Poochie?

"It's the only name he comes to," explained Marisa, our youngest child and only daughter. So Poochie it was, at least for a few months. For by then there was a death in the family, and everything changed.

The languid days of summer turtled by, seemingly in no hurry to bring us to September. Poochie thrived. Lonely for the four dogs we left at home, the children lavished attention on this perfect playmate. Never once did the dog set foot inside the house, but as we lived on our lanai, he wasn't shorted for company.

The three boys, Larry, Mitch, and Bryan, took leg-flying runs along the beach in front of our home, with Poochie keeping up rather well. They played tag; they hid from him. He and our daughter scrambled up any slightly leaning tree, this nine-year-old girl and the poi dog, grinning down at those of us who were not part monkey. This doggy person was happy. The only game the little fellow would not play was "fetch the stick." The minute anyone picked up a stick to throw, Poochie would cringe and slump pathetically, waiting for the blows that would never come from our hands.

He had one very unusual talent. He could husk and eat a coconut faster than it takes to tell you. Any fresh fallen coconut from one of our backyard trees was fair game, and he would hold it firmly between his front paws, and with those sharp teeth, peel away the skin, getting right down to the meat and the milk. He taught Marisa how to do this, and it is no easy task. Thank goodness she didn't use her teeth.

A phone call early in the morning of August 23 brought our carefree summer to an abrupt end. My husband's mother had died in Sacramento. The funeral could be held off for a few days, but we must pack up and return to the mainland as soon as possible.

Chaos everywhere. Suitcases and clothes and surfboards came out, and each one of us was crying. The dear lady who had just passed away from our lives was very much loved. Poor little Poochie followed us from car to front door and back again—a dejected soul with worried eyes. Poochie. How could we go home and leave our poi dog to wait alone on the big lanai for our car that would never come up the drive; for his family who were not coming back? We couldn't.

"No, no, no," my husband shook his head for emphasis. "We have four dogs already, and that's two too many in my opinion. We are not keeping Poochie."

All right then, we'd find him a good home. But a few frantic phone calls to friends in Hawaii proved futile; they had their quota of dogs and did not want another. The children and I racked our brains to think of someone on the mainland who would take Poochie. No dice.

And then the names of Dan and Dee popped into my head. A couple in their mid-thirties, they were loving and warm and a lot of fun. They had no children or pets, and best of all, they worked for my mother and lived on her large property, so Poochie would have room to run and we could see him. It was decided that someone should phone them right away and tell them that what they really needed to make their lives complete was a Hawaiian poi dog. I was elected to make the call. I rehearsed carefully what I would say, practiced in front of my family, and then picked up the phone.

They agreed! It didn't even require my super-duper sales pitch.

"What does he look like?" asked Dan.

"Is he smart and wonderful?" Dee wanted to know. "Can you get him out of Hawaii and into California?"

We hadn't thought of that. Getting a dog into Hawaii is close to impossible and requires six months of quarantine. But going the other way? A phone call was directed to Animal Control. No problem. Get a vet's certificate that he'd had all his shots and then call the airline and reserve a kennel. We did. The idea of taking Poochie in a car was a new one for him, but he hopped in and rode along with good cheer. The vet deemed him to be about a year old and in good health. The airlines moved our reservation up and held a kennel for us. Two mornings after that phone call we were all off to the Honolulu airport.

How we worried about stuffing Poi Dog into that kennel. We needn't have. He walked in like a champ, turned around, and lay down as the door clanged shut. How we worried about the five-hour flight to the mainland and the noise and the vibration. How would a half-wild dog from the beaches of Hawaii survive such a trip? I'll tell you how he survived it. This scene has stayed in my mind for all of these years, and it will always remain.

Into the crowded baggage claim area at LAX came Poochie's kennel. Bryan opened his door and out stepped Poochie. He shook himself. He stretched himself. And then he stood proudly, and he quietly surveyed his surroundings.

"So this is L.A.," he seemed to be thinking. "Noisy, isn't it?"

By now a crowd was gathering and people were murmuring: "Oh, what a beautiful dog!" and "What kind is he?" and "Isn't he well behaved?" and things like that. Just about bursting with pride, my children informed one and all that here stood a genuine Hawaiian poi dog in the flesh. Although my eyes were misty, I saw him clearly as I see him today. Yes, he was smart and wonderful and kind, but he was more. Poochie was handsome. The months of care had filled him out, and his coat shone in the lights of the airport. With all the grace in the world he allowed us to snap on his red leash.

And as he trotted out into the cool, foggy night, I wondered if he knew of the life that lay ahead of him; knew that Dan and Dee would name him Kimo and would move to a house on the beach; that he would live to be seventeen years old and the delight of everyone whose path he crossed; that he would come to be known as "Kimo, awesome dog of Carpinteria."

I think he did. I really do.

Poi dog canis familiaris

In Hawaii dogs were kept as pets, for food, as items of barter, and for sacrifice. They were prominent in sorcery and folklore.

Charlie

H e came to me the way so many of them did, a silent little lump of gray down, big feet, big bill, not one feather yet. And I turned to the children, who were wearing their hopeful faces, and I said what I always said: "What on earth am I supposed to do with this?"

"Just hold him in your hands and make him well, Mom, you know, like you do."

I could feel the heart beating way too fast, and I cupped one hand over the other to keep him warm. But oh—such a faint beat. And he was so wet.

"Where did you find him, in the pool?" I wanted to know.

"We took him away from Max, Mom. That old dog was going to

eat him. We looked for a nest or a worried mother bird, but we were in the middle of the pasture. We'll go get the cage so he'll have a place to sleep tonight."

And they were gone, leaving *this* worried mother bird alone with a handful of frightened fluff. Judging from his heart flutters, I doubted that he would live to see the night.

He proved me wrong. By bedtime the little heart was beating slowly and steadily and the baby bird had nestled into my palm for the night. Usually, we would line a small box with Kleenex, plop the fledgling in it, put it under a light in the bathroom, and close the door. This time I didn't do that; I can't tell you why. Taking the tiny fellow into our bed, I stuffed him up under my armpit and then spent the entire night trying not to roll over and squish him. By morning my bed-bird was quite chipper. I was exhausted. Rallying the children to the cause, I ordered:

"Larry, go find the eyedropper. Mitch, get the Gerber's Baby Meat from the pantry. This little fella is ready for breakfast."

For a bird so young I made a gruel out of baby food and water and eyedroppered it down his throat. As the days went by I rolled the baby meat in my fingers to make "worms," and he gobbled them straight with a water chaser. He thrived. He graduated to real worms and he grew. We named him Charlie. Feathers began to appear, and as they did, he would sit in his cage and flap his wings.

Soon he would be strong and we would return him to the wild. That's what we thought.

One afternoon I opened Charlie's cage, and he flew right at my face, trying unsuccessfully to perch on my nose.

He fell off onto my shirt and scrambled up onto my shoulder. And there he stayed. From dawn to dusk Charlie rode everywhere I went, in the car or in the house. Taking him outside, I would point to the birds darting about the spring sky.

"Look, Charlie. See them go? That's where you belong, up there flying free."

I'd put him on my finger and launch him. He was agreeable enough. He'd fly little circles around my head, always coming back to perch on my shoulder. And he'd chirp. Freely translated, his chirps meant: "Can we go in now? I'm hungry."

Charlie became a full-grown Western grasshopper sparrow, and he took his place as a funny, lively, and cheeky member of our family. His favorite time of day was "martini time." He had been sitting on my shoulder one evening as I sipped on a drink and munched some crackers. Absently, I dunked a bit of cracker in my martini and offered it to Charlie, who gobbled it right down. That was it. Charlie was hooked. Things reached the point where he would anticipate the cocktail hour and at exactly 5:00 P.M. he would land on the counter underneath the cupboard

where we kept the cocktail glasses, and he would hop up and down until I selected a glass. Then he would fly ahead of me across the room to the armoire that held our liquor. Preceding me once again, he would return to the counter where I built my martini, impatiently peeping and hopping until I was ready for the crackers. These he would practically pull out of the box. Once in my easy chair, Charlie on my shoulder, cocktail hour could begin.

What ended it for Charlie was the way he behaved. After his "nip" the bird would fly to the highest rafter of our ceiling and look around for the cat. We owned, at the time, a beautiful Siamese named Shere-Khan, who had to be the most laid-back cat in the animal kingdom. Although field mice scampered into our Solvang home, Shere-Khan would not deign to catch or, Heaven forbid, kill one. Beneath his station, you know. He regally tolerated babies, children, dogs, and even other cats. He politely tolerated Charlie.

But once Charlie had had his martini, he would dive-bomb that cat like a tiny Stuka, swooping low over his back and up between his ears on his way back to the rafters. Often he would leave a little calling card between the cat's ears. After several of these attacks, poor Shere-Khan would crawl behind a chair or under the table to get away from that swacked sparrow. So shortly, we substituted water-dipped crackers for Charlie's martini.

One evening we had a dinner party. As we seated ourselves in the dining room, Charlie zoomed in looking for me. In those days I wore my hair long, and for this occasion I had it up in a bun on top of my head. Charlie landed on my head instead of my shoulder, and he didn't get down. Seconds later I felt a tug on my hair and little bird feet marching around on top of my scalp. As our guests collapsed with laughter, Charlie rearranged my bun to his liking and then settled down in his "nest," where he remained for the rest of the evening.

Every dinner was a dinner party at my mother's house. No matter how few people sat at her table, the meal was served in courses with crystal finger bowls brought in before the dessert course.

One evening my mother, her nurse, Carol, and my family sat down to supper. Charlie was snugly ensconced in my bun atop my head. When the finger bowls arrived on the table, Charlie let out a joyful peep and sailed off my head and onto the white damask tablecloth. Hopping smartly up to my mother's finger bowl, he plopped his fat little bird body into the warm lemon-scented water.

"For me?" he chirped happily. "You shouldn't have."

Mom's hand was over her mouth while tears of laughter fell from her eyes. The rest of us just sat dumbly and watched as Charlie took his bath in the finger bowl, dipping and splashing, cheeping and bowing. When he was quite clean, he flopped his sodden feathered form onto the tablecloth and then he shook himself. Droplets of

water hit the Steuben candlesticks, the Meissen candy dishes, the Spode china settings. Well, he made a mess is what he did. But we were all roaring with laughter, and no one cared.

We had rented a home in Kahuku, Hawaii, that summer of 1975, and we left California the middle of June. We left without Charlie. Intending to take him with us, I had punched some holes in the top of a candy tin and coaxed Charlie inside to a nest of soft rags. Putting the lid on securely, we weren't even out the door before frantic squawks emanated from the tin. Charlie lay on the bottom of his

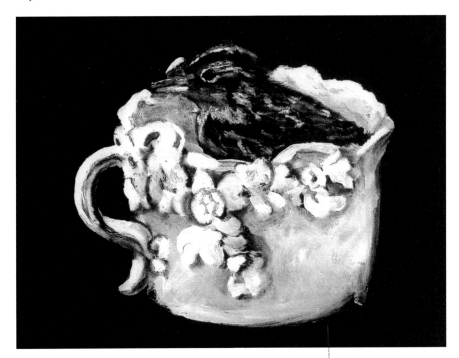

"nest," wild-eyed with fright, his heart pounding. He would never have survived the five-hour flight to Hawaii. We left him at my mother's house with Carol, whom he adored, and with instructions to keep him separate from Carol's Cairn terrier and Mom's Boston terrier.

We had been in Hawaii nearly a week with no phone call from Carol. Very strange. One day my husband and children drove into Honolulu, and I elected to stay home with our poi dog. I was feeling uneasy, and it was with a sense of foreboding that I picked up the phone and called the mainland. The minute I heard Carol's voice I knew that Charlie was dead.

"How did it happen?" I asked woodenly.

"Oh, Tita, I'm so sorry," Carol burst into tears. "Your mother and I were asked over to the Awl's for dinner. Before we left we put Charlie in his cage on a low table by the window and locked the dogs in the other room. We told the maid not to open the door between the two rooms under any circumstance, but she didn't listen. When she went in to turn down the bed, our two dogs ran into Charlie's room and knocked his cage off the table. Oh, Tita, poor Charlie died of fright."

I don't recall hanging up the phone or leaving the house. I just remember the sand under the soles of my feet and the tears streaming down my cheeks. I walked and walked and walked— walked until the anger dissipated, walked until the pain dulled to an ache, walked until my grief slowly gave way to hopelessness. And when I could walk no further, I sat down upon the sand and looked out to the sea. I asked it one question: "Why?"

My answer rolled in with the next wave, and this is what it was:

"Charlie lived a very short life, but while he lived he was loved; while he lived, he was happy. You can't ask more than that for a little bird."

You can't ask more than that for any of us.

Shark

I got him."

Ami was looking at me, a wide smile creasing his face, his teeth dazzling white against the chocolate brown skin.

"Lolita," his soft voice stretched out my name, "come here."

"What have you got, Ami?" I was standing next to him now, peering into the brilliant and clear blue water.

"The shark, Lolita," he grinned. "The big one."

"Really? How big do you think?"

He jigged his fishing line a few times, but it appeared to be caught on the bottom. And then he said: "Six hundred pounds."

"Oh, right." I tried to keep my smile from becoming a laugh, and I took a seat somewhat behind him so he would not see my

amusement. How these Fijian natives loved to tease me. Such a lighthearted, carefree people they were.

This was Malolo Lai Lai Island off the coast of Fiji and about a ten-minute plane ride from Nadi. My husband and I and our four children had come here from our home in New Zealand. We were spending ten days at a very rustic resort on this seven-by-three-mile island—little thatched huts along a white sand beach, very few amenities and no entertainment—that sort of rustic. We were having the time of our lives. The big adventure of the day was to ride out to sea in the garbage scow and watch the garbage go overboard and perhaps catch a few of the fish who had come to scavenge.

And so on that bright, sunny first day of June in 1977 our family climbed aboard a twenty-foot open boat with a dozen other guests, and at 8:15 A.M. we took on barrels of garbage and off we went. Three native men guided our boat to a place where the reef dropped away and the water became very deep. John, Ami, and his brother, Watson, began tossing garbage into the ocean. Within seconds fish swarmed around the boat and fishing lines went over the side.

A Coca-Cola bottle floated briefly on the surface of the sea, and I watched as it slowly filled with water and began to sink. All of a sudden I saw a huge shape zoom upwards, eat the Coca-Cola bottle, and vanish almost before I could register what it was.

"What was that?" I gasped.

"Shark," replied Watson. "We will fish for him."

Of course he's joking, I thought. That thing was enormous. But I watched with growing wonder as he took out a hook the size of an anchor, loaded it with raw meat, and handed it to Ami, who lowered it over the side, holding onto the heavy fish line with his bare hands. It didn't seem that much time passed before I saw Ami give his line a sharp upward jerk. And then that smile lit up his face as he told me he had hooked the shark.

Directly after this announcement, Watson pulled the fish line through Ami's left hand, looped it across his back and over his shoulder, bringing it out through Ami's right hand. In this way, Ami could use his body as a fulcrum and yet let go of the line if he had to.

The bubbles in my held-up laughter began to fizzle out. My God! They were serious!

"Ami," I was at his side again, "what do you do now that you've hooked a six-hundred-pound shark?" I looked around the small boat and felt a twinge of apprehension.

"I drown him, Lolita." He loved saying my name. "You see, shark must move all the time, never stop. And he does not swim backward. So I hold him in one place, jig him up and down and drown him. Then I pull him in."

I was fascinated. "How long does this take? Do you catch many sharks?"

"Takes about two hour, maybe more. We catch a shark maybe one every two months." Ami was pulling up on and then releasing his line. He inclined his head toward a basket of fruit. "You getting hungry? Want something to eat?" he asked.

I shook my head. "No," I smiled. "I'll wait for your shark." But I wasn't laughing now.

The morning passed by pleasantly enough. The children were catching suckerfish, long dark fish that the natives cooked up for us for dinner. They were delicious.

Sometime after the first hour Ami informed me that he had been wrong about the shark weighing six hundred pounds. Well, of course he was wrong, I thought. But when he said the shark was eight hundred pounds, I grew very quiet as I listened to the passengers speculate about the shark down there in the deep being drowned by a skillful Fijian native.

"Here he comes," cried out Ami, and we all rushed to his side of the boat. Not smart. The boat tipped dangerously, and we were redistributed at once. Out came the cameras, and we peered into the ocean straining for the first glimpse. The water was still; nothing was there.

Suddenly, the water began to churn and boil, and then the shark was there. He was everywhere. The water was filled with him; the boat lurched and heaved from the waves he created. He was simply colossal and big and mad as he fought and dove and surfaced and lunged. He swam straight at our boat and tore a hole in the side where I was holding onto my seat. Luckily the hole was above the waterline.

No one was on Ami's side of the boat now; we gave him room as we watched in awe how well he played that fish. Even tired and half dead, that shark was awesome. He looked like every shark in every picture I had ever seen—mean and ugly with small horrid eyes and all mouth. A shark has several rows of teeth in his jaws that he can rotate forward and pull back, much as a cat can unsheathe its claws. All rows were forward now, and he was turning his head from side to side, slashing at the air. He was making a strange hissing sound too; a kind of inverted gasp. We stayed at a safe distance, if safe there could be on such a tiny boat, and we waited, snapping pictures all the while.

A tall fishing boat from the resort came alongside with the owner on board. He saw the drama that was unfolding, and he reached for a rifle, a .22-cailber. As Ami brought the shark in close, the owner fired: pop, pop, pop. He pumped seventeen bullets into the shark, but the animal wasn't fazed. He just got madder. A grappling hook was brought out to pin the fish to the side of the boat. He ate the grappling hook. Chomp. It was gone.

After a good half-hour, an exciting half-hour, the shark was spent. The natives had him so wrapped in line he could barely move. As he sagged against the boat, they tied him alongside tail first so that as we sped through the water, it would not rush into his gills and revive him. We headed for our island. The shark was still.

Thinking he was dead and as he was tied right next to my seat, I decided to examine him closely. I wondered what he felt like to the touch, so I ran my hand along his dorsal fin. Weird. If I stroked it upwards it felt like velvet, but going the other way it was like sandpaper. I heard that terrible intake of breath, and as I threw myself across the boat, the shark's jaws snapped shut where my hand had been a second before. Dazed, I looked up into Ami's troubled eyes.

"Close, Lolita, close."

We brought the shark back to Malolo Lai Lai and hauled him onto the beach. He was an eight-hundred-pound bronze whaler, and he measured nine and a half feet in length.

A crowd had gathered, keeping a respectful distance from the shark. I stood beside Watson.

"What now?" I asked my native friend. "What will become of him?"

"In Fiji, Lolita, nothing is wasted," he smiled at me. "We take out garbage and dump it at the edge of the reef. The fish eat our garbage.

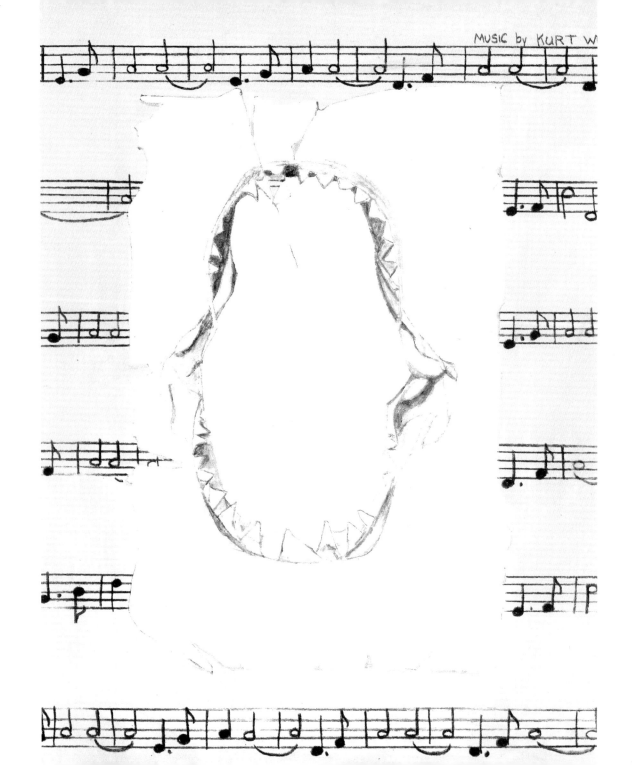

We eat the fish. Big shark like this, we take half of him back to the village and make feast for many days. We celebrate because we have rid the waters of a killer. The other half we send to the cat food factory in Nadi for feeding people's pet cats. You see, nothing is wasted."

"I wonder who gets the half with the Coca-Cola bottle," I laughed.

Several of the guests offered Ami a lot of money for the shark's jaws, but he declined. And then a lovely thing happened. Our family left the resort three days after catching the shark, and as we were leaving our hut, Ami, Watson, and John appeared bearing a strange-looking package. It was the shark's jaws wrapped in newspaper, minus one large tooth that Ami was wearing around his neck. It was proudly presented to my husband. There were a lot of hugs and kisses and tears. I will never forget Malolo Lai Lai Island or the kind and loving Fijian people.

I will also never forget the speed with which we were shot through customs in Hawaii a few hours later. Apparently, a few pieces of flesh were still hanging on in between the shark's teeth. As the wrapped-up jaws came down the conveyor belt from the plane's cargo hold, the stench was overwhelming. We were shown the door, and we arrived in the United States at a dizzying pace.

Hercules

$\mathcal{I}$t had been one of *those* days. Everything that could have gone wrong did, and five o'clock found me sinking into my favorite easy chair with an ice-cold martini in hand. Bryan burst into the room, face aglow, and announced: "Mom, Hercules is here. He's out on the pool terrace. Come look."

Ten-year-old Bryan and two of the neighbor boys had walked into our town, Solvang, to play on the school grounds and had just returned.

"Bryan," I said warily, "if Hercules has four legs and a tail, get him out of here. Take him back where you found him."

"Aw, Mom, we tried, but he followed us home. He won't go back—Dad!" He was running down the hall to his father's study.

35

"Dad, come see Hercules."

Moments later one half of my husband edged around the door leading from the pool terrace. He had a look of awe on his face.

"Honey, you really should come outside and see this."

"You mean get up?" I grumbled. But I was already out of my chair.

He stood on the lawn next to the swimming pool. He was one of the most magnificent animals I have ever seen in my life. Now, I think basset hounds are funny looking, but I know a show dog when I see one, and this dog had "champion" stamped all over him. The sun was low in the sky, and its long golden rays spotlighted a coat that glistened like patent leather. He was jet black where he was black and dazzling white in contrast. He had a caramel-colored head with long velvety brown ears.

My first feeling was one of relief. Hercules would not be joining our family of four children, three dogs, one Siamese cat, seven hens, two horses, and a sheep. Someone must be frantically searching for him. We found it hard to believe that he had no collar on his neck. My second thought was that you don't turn a dog like this out on the street. It was agreed that we would give Hercules some supper and a bed for the night, but bright and early the next morning we would try to locate the owner.

The dog's bed of choice was Bryan's, and later that night my husband once again told me I must go with him to see something.

Bryan was all covered up in bed, sound asleep, his head on his pillow. Next to him, asleep with his head resting on the other pillow, was Hercules.

The next day was Monday. Solvang's local paper came out early on Thursdays, so I phoned the Society for the Prevention of Cruelty to Animals and the sheriff's office to see if anyone had reported a missing basset hound. No one had. Next, calls went out to the four veterinarians in the Valley. Three families owned basset hounds, but no one had lost one. I walked to town with Hercules on a leash and asked in at homes near the schoolyard and even at stores. Nothing. It would seem that this beautiful dog had dropped out of nowhere.

Imagine our surprise on Thursday when our newspaper carried no ad for a missing basset hound. No one was looking for Hercules. So I put in an ad that would come out the following Thursday: "Found in Solvang, basset hound. Owner please call 868-4636 and identify."

In the eleven days that we kept Hercules, the dog thoroughly captivated our family. What a charming, funny animal. He adored me. Basset hounds adore everyone, but I didn't know that at the time. He got along amazingly well with our other dogs, and even the Siamese cat made friends with him. But Bryan was his. It didn't take eleven days for us to see that a bond was being forged between those two that was not meant to be broken.

And so on Thursday the local newspaper hit the stands, my family went to school and work, and I stayed near the phone and worried. The call came late in the afternoon.

"You've got my dog," a voice said over the line in reply to my, "Hello."

"Oh, really?" I said, most unpleasantly. "What does the dog look like?"

"Well, he's just your ordinary basset hound," he began. But the man got no further.

"Oh, no, he's not," I snapped. "He's the most beautiful dog I've seen; he looks like a show dog. You could never call *this* dog ordinary."

"Oh, well, yes, he is—a show dog, I mean. He won all his puppy classes and then won his first adult class and went on to win best of breed. I have his trophy and ribbons."

"Good God," I exploded. "Do you mean to tell me that you have lost a valuable show dog, have made no attempt to find him, and have just left him to wander the streets for eleven days?"

I was beside myself with anger and continued to verbally pulverize this dreadful dog owner for a good five minutes. When he finally got a chance to speak, he offered this explanation:

The man's name was Ted. The dog was called George. Ted and his roommate raised and showed cocker spaniels and had just moved from Los Angeles to Solvang. They had bought the basset as a gift for Ted's sister, who lived in Lompoc with three children. But the children abused the dog. Ted could not bear to see George's ears fastened atop his head with clothespins or to see Q-tips sticking out of his nose. As the sister did nothing to intervene on the dog's behalf, Ted took George back.

"So, you see, when the dog ran away last week, we really didn't look for him very hard. We sort of prayed that he had found a good home," Ted finished lamely.

"I'll buy him from you."

The words were out of my mouth before I realized I'd said them.

There was a pause. "Well, I can't do that because my sister said she wants George back as soon as she gets her yard fenced. Can I come over and get him now?"

"No," I burst out. "I mean, he isn't here. He, uh—my husband had to take one of our kids over to Santa Barbara, and the dog went along for the ride. And, let's see, they won't be back until late tonight, so that would not be convenient. How about tomorrow?"

I was lying. The children were lined up beside my chair wearing pinched faces, and Hercules was laying on the floor being strangely quiet. I needed time.

"Well," Ted said, sounding put out, "I work, so I couldn't come over until after four tomorrow, and I'm going to Los

Angeles after that for the weekend. I'll just come by to be sure it's George."

Good. The arrangements were made, and I hung up the phone. I had to think of something and I had to think fast. I thought of something.

Now, what I did next will be embarrassing to tell you because in the telling you will learn what a deceptive, dishonest, and determined wretch I can be when pushed to it. Just bear in mind one thing: I had *no* intention of giving *that* dog back to *that* man—or to the children with the clothespins and the Q-tips.

After a short family conference I phoned Becky. Becky was a friend of mine who lived in the neighboring town of Santa Ynez. She had a noble basset hound. He was a male, and his name was Beauregard. Becky loved dogs. She listened with growing outrage as my tale unfolded, and of course, she agreed at once to my outrageous plan.

And so on Friday morning Hercules and I drove over to Becky's house. Beauregard and I came back.

Beau and the children were out of sight when Ted rang our doorbell at four o'clock. I opened the door, and then I wished the ground could open up and swallow me. On my doorstep stood a nice looking young man. In his left hand he held a silver trophy. Between his fingers several blue ribbons were sticking out. In his right hand was the familiar parchment paper rolled up and tied with a ribbon. He was bringing me George/Hercules's prizes and pedigree. It could mean only one thing. I could not speak.

"Well," said Ted. "I called my sister last night, and I told her that George was living with a lady who sounded like she sure didn't want to give him up. My sister said she had put fifty dollars' worth of food into the dog and if that lady wanted George, she would have to pay fifty dollars."

Ted looked at me. He had large, sincere brown eyes. "I would have made you a present of George, Mrs. Lanning. If you don't mind paying fifty dollars . . ."

I felt sick. Forcing a weak smile, I invited Ted in.

"How nice of you, Ted," I said. "Maybe we'd better let the dog in and see if it is really your George."

As the children and Beauregard streamed into the house, Beau made a beeline for Ted and adored him on the spot. But a look of genuine anguish crossed Ted's face.

"Oh, that's not my dog," he cried. "That's not George. Oh, I'm so sorry!"

His sorrow couldn't compare to mine. To this day the rest of our visit remains a blur. I remember him picking up the trophy, ribbons, and pedigree and going out the door looking like a deflated balloon. He was on his way to Los Angeles and would be back Sunday, and he gave me his phone number in Solvang just in case I might hear something about George. And then he was gone.

I stood dumbfounded, avoiding the eyes of my children. "Oh, what a tangled web we weave. . . ." How was I going to untangle this one? All the way back out to Becky's house, Beauregard by my side, I pondered but could think of nothing other than to tell Ted the truth, and that was unthinkable.

Becky came up with the idea, not a very good one, but better than anything I had, so I headed back to Solvang with Hercules. "Make it so complicated it will be impossible to follow," Becky had said, "and maybe he will believe you." Trouble is, I was having trouble following it, and I rehearsed her brainstorm over and over during the weekend.

I made the call Monday afternoon. Ted had just come home from work. Here is the story I spun for him:

I had a friend in Santa Ynez called Becky, and she had a basset hound named Beauregard. About a week ago, Beau had wandered off and Becky had been looking for him, calling everyone she knew to tell them of her loss. One of her friends heard of Becky's plight and called to tell her that she had found a basset hound wandering around Solvang. It must be

Beauregard. She brought the dog over to Becky, but it wasn't her basset. Of course not, because Beau had followed my children home and was with us, as Ted had seen.

Becky kept the basset temporarily, however, as her friend had three cats who hated dogs. Becky didn't get an ad into the local paper in time for Thursday's issue, but she saw mine and phoned me as soon as she read the paper, which didn't happen until Friday evening, as she had been away on business Thursday. She came right over to my house, and a joyful reunion took place when she saw Beauregard.

Then I told her about you, Ted, and your missing George. We knew you were in L.A. so Becky agreed to leave the unknown basset with me until I could reach you.

"Ted," I finished my saga with my fingers crossed, "how many basset hounds could be walking the streets of Solvang? And this dog is a beaut. It has to be George. Can you believe this?" I was praying that he could.

He did.

"Oh, I hope you have George, Mrs. Lanning. I can hardly believe—*two* basset hounds—can I come right over?"

Ten minutes later Ted was again at my door but without the ribbons and trophy. Oh, oh! The children and George/Hercules spilled into the room, and the dog greeted his master with a big tail wag and then went over to Bryan.

I suggested we all sit down and talk. We told Ted that in the three days we had had George we had grown very attached to him, especially Bryan, and that we would like to buy him and keep him with us if the offer was still good. Ted, sitting at one end of our couch, was silent. Hercules had jumped up beside him, and right next to Hercules was Bryan. The room was very quiet.

And then Hercules did something that sealed his fate. He looked up into Ted's face for a long moment. He turned and settled himself across Bryan's lap and gave a sigh you could hear in San Francisco.

Ted's eyes met mine and he smiled. "It looks like George is home," he said.

It has been said about basset hounds that if you lowered their I.Q. by three points, they would be dumber than an after-dinner mint. In the eight years that Hercules shared his life with us I was never tempted to rename him Einstein, but he was not dumb. He had the brains to follow Bryan home. I'd call him street smart. He also had a sense of humor.

He loved to play hide-and-seek. When he decided it was his turn to hide, he would take himself off as fast as his stubby legs could carry

him and he would find a tree or a bush to get behind. You could call and call his name, but he stayed "hidden," often his hind end sticking out, until you came looking for him. If you weren't quick about it, Herc would peek around his barrier to see if you were coming.

And he loved to be chased, even taking his turn chasing the children. If they pretended to be frightened, all the better, and Hercules would end up on his back fairly wriggling with delight. Gentle of disposition, he was happy, game, and an inspired playmate.

About a year after acquiring Herc, we moved from Solvang. Ted was still telling anyone who would listen about the lady who found not one but *two* basset hounds in the Santa Ynez Valley.

Our house in Montecito boasted an elevator that went from an entry room to the bedrooms upstairs. We never used it, preferring to climb the stairs instead. When Bryan was thirteen years old, he underwent surgery for a slipped epiphysis and came home from St. John's Hospital in Santa Monica with two steel pins in his hip and a pair of crutches. The elevator proved invaluable in getting our son upstairs to his room. Hercules was delighted with this alternative to stair climbing and never missed a trip up or down.

Not more than a month after Bryan's surgery, Hercules took himself off for a walk along Cold Spring Road after dinner. He was hit by a car. Cut to the bone, his flank was laid open like a sardine can. His legs, too, were cut to ribbons and were useless. But the hound managed to drag himself over a quarter of a mile to our doorstep, where he keened for help.

Back from the vet, we unloaded the dog's bandages, extra tubes, and such when Bryan asked: "Where's Herc?"

"What do you mean where's Herc? He's in the back of the station wagon," I replied confidently. We'd lowered him in.

"No, he's not, Mom. I just looked."

We were frantic. Somehow that big basset had slipped out of the car while we were unloading it and was hobbling around our property. A search began that ended a bit later in gales of laughter. Hercules was found sitting in the elevator, patiently waiting for someone to take him up to his and Bryan's room. No after-dinner mint here.

Basset hounds are by nature gregarious. They love people and they love to be the center of attention. With four school-age children, a menagerie of animals, and an invalid grandmother to look after, we were busy and could not give the dog our undivided attention.

But our home was across the street from Westmont College, and one day, a bored Hercules lumbered across Cold Spring Road and went to college. So began a seven-year love affair between Hercules and the Westmont students. He was ecstatic with all the petting and attention. And the college kids just plain loved this big, affable hound. Whenever the dog was missing from our yard, we

would drive onto the Westmont campus and ask the nearest student: "Have you seen Hercules?"

The answer would always be: "Oh, yeah, he's up in Dorm B" or "I just saw him at the Student Center." And we would find him surrounded by his college friends, basking in their affection.

One day we received a phone call from the dean of students at Westmont. The college was going to perform *The Wizard of* Oz at the County Bowl in Santa Barbara. Could they borrow Hercules for a few nights?

"Hercules? Whatever for?" my husband asked.

"Well, we want him to be Toto," came the reply.

Because Herc bore no resemblance whatsoever to a Cairn terrier, the students made a sign that fit over the dog's back and hung down on both sides. On it was written one word: TOTO. When our basset sauntered amiably on stage, the audience went wild. Needless to say, he stole the show.

Always a lean dog, it was hard to say when Herc first began to lose weight. I noticed it in May of his ninth year. But our vet could find nothing wrong. By mid-June his ribs began to show prominently, and we took him to a different vet. A battery of tests followed, and a few days later the vet called us in for a talk.

"Herc has cancer," he told us. "It looks like it started in his liver, but by now it has spread everywhere. I'm so sorry."

Hercules Lanning

For the next few weeks we kept our dear friend close by us. He slept a lot but otherwise seemed no worse for wear. And then one day in early July he could not eat. He was hungry and wagged all over when his food dish was placed in front of him. He tried to eat, but he could not swallow. I knew the cancer had reached his throat. I tried hand-feeding him, but the food would not go down.

"It has to be now," I thought. Hercules was still vital, still alert. In a few days he wouldn't be. My husband agreed with my decision, and he phoned our vet and said the terrible words. He was to bring the dog right in. We had prepared Bryan for this day. No one had prepared me.

I said good-bye to Herc. There on the floor of my bedroom I stroked his long, velvety ears for the last time and told him that I loved him. Told him how glad I was that he had come into my life, how he had brightened it. My husband called his name, and Hercules jumped to his feet. He walked out of my room; he walked out of my life looking just the way he had eight years before when I first saw him standing on our terrace in Solvang—head up, tail awag. I wanted him to go out proud, and he did. Oh, he did!

Owl Talk

$\mathcal{I}$ stand in awe of them, these feathered giants, the great horned owls. Impressive in size and sound, they have no natural enemies, are strangers to fear, and dominate the night with their cunning and their cry. I had the good luck not only to get to know these magnificent creatures but to be befriended by them. This is how it happened.

In the summer of 1967, my family and I moved back into the house where I was raised. Built by my grandparents in 1919, it was situated on fifty-five heavily wooded acres in Montecito, California. There was a grove of stately Kentia palm trees to one side of the house, many massive oaks scattered around our residence, and an enormous stand of eucalyptus trees just below us.

As a child I used to lie in bed and listen to the owls calling to one another, and so it was with no surprise that on our very first night in that old house, I once again heard the familiar "who-whoo-whoo-whoo" outside my window. Who indeed? The house had been vacant for over two years, so the horned owls must have had undisturbed nights to scoop up the big palm rats that lived in the Kentia grove. Now lights streamed from porch and window and people moved about. Surely the owls were curious. What was happening to their haunt?

"Oh, Mom, come look!" It was our oldest son, Larry, and he was staring out of our family room window. "That's the biggest owl I've ever seen."

For there, perched on a branch in an oak tree not twenty feet from our lighted porch, was a great horned owl. No doubt we had invaded his territory, for he came night after night and, when not looking noble, would lower his head and peer in the windows to see what we were about.

Now, anything wild that comes near me gets fed. But what to feed a great horned owl?

"They prey on live rats, mice, rabbits, gophers, chipmunks, and squirrels," our veterinarian informed me.

Well, having no live rats, mice, rabbits, chipmunks, gophers, or squirrels in my larder, I rolled up a piece of raw hamburger and threw it along the porch. The owl watched it with interest, but as soon as it stopped rolling, he turned his large yellow eyes on me as if to say: "Would you have any hasenpfeffer?"

Frustrated that I could not feed him, I decided to sit outside on the porch and talk to him. On nights when weather would permit and the children had been tucked in, I would do just that.

"What a fine fellow you are," I crooned to the owl as I gazed admiringly at my huge friend, beautifully dressed in demure grays, browns, buffs, and whites, with eyes the color of meerschaum. "Such pretty eyes, and look at your great, long ears." My glance had shifted to the prominent tufts of gray-white feathers on either side of his head that give the great horned owl his distinctive appearance. "My! You are a beauty."

The owl never made a sound but stared his unblinking stare and seemed to be thinking important thoughts.

As the days of summer passed, he became comfortable with my presence and would move about on the oak branch, turning his head around, no longer keeping an eye on me. At the time, I had no idea that the owl and I were bonding, nor how deep that bond would go. I was soon to find out.

Our bedroom was upstairs above the family room and facing the giant oak where the owl sat. The room had large windows on three sides, and one night while I sat reading in bed, my daughter, Marisa, came into the room.

"I see you've got a friend," she chuckled.

Lowering my book to gaze out the window, I looked right into the eyes of the owl. He had moved to a higher branch in the oak so he could see into our bedroom. After that he would supervise my bedtime routine. His was a comforting presence, and often my last image before closing my eyes was of that majestic owl watching over me.

"Mom, come to the window!" Marisa cried one night as I was washing up for bed. "There are two of them. Our owl has brought a friend."

And sure enough, he had. For next to our owl sat a smaller one, still impressive in size but more feminine looking. We guessed that she was his mate. We guessed right. Now in the night came an answering hoot to his call as the two owls hunted and chatted until dawn brightened the sky.

The months passed; the owls remained. We settled into the house and looked forward to nocturnal visits. At times we felt like people inside a television set, going about our evening's entertainment, while outside, peering through the window panes, sat the owls, thoroughly enjoying the show.

By the end of February, the calls of the male and female owl intensified and there was much activity in and around a giant eucalyptus

tree close by our house near the tennis court. The owls were building a nest and were going to raise a family. Not long after, we trained our binoculars on the huge nest and had our first glimpse of the new arrivals. Two whitish-gray heads were peeking over the edge of the twigs.

We watched them grow. Big, soft, downy owlets at first, their fuzz was soon replaced by feathers. And one evening, Mother Owl decided it was time for the babes to try their wings. We took ringside seats by the tennis court and watched their solo flight. The first part was easy. Mother Owl simply pushed junior out of the nest, and with a graceful glide he made it safely to the ground, followed by his sibling.

Then the fun began, for even a baby owl is heavy and his wings not very strong yet. And so they hopped and flopped and did a few clumsy crashes, gaining a little altitude and losing a lot. They finally perched upon a woodpile under their tree, looked embarrassed, and tried to pretend they weren't there. Walking up to them, I got to within petting distance while they turned away their heads and averted their eyes. Only my respect for the parent owls halted my steps, and I left the children untouched. Eventually, with much flapping and fuss, the young ones flew from limb to limb on the tree, finally making it all the way up to their nest. We cheered.

At dusk Mother Owl would bring her babies down to sit on a wooden archway beside the tennis court. And one summer's eve, as we were admiring mother and babies, one of our children tossed a tennis ball out onto the court. The little owls were all attention as they watched the ball bounce along. Then suddenly—swoosh—one owlet pounced on that ball, picked it up in his talons, and proudly flew back to his mother. Unable to perch and hold onto his "prey" at the same time, the baby made a wild loop-the-loop around the archway before he dropped the tennis ball, grabbed at his perch, and came to rest upside down, hanging onto the rail for dear life and looking totally chagrined.

Great horned owls mate for life, and so year after year, they would fill the night with their calls and, after much discussion, would always return to the same nest, remodel it, and raise their young. Sometimes two, sometimes three little owls would pounce on tennis balls for practice, but would quickly abandon the game when they tried to eat a Dunlop Three Star.

Apparently, owl families stay together, too, even after the young grow up. For in the twenty years we occupied that old house, our big oak by the porch saw its branches fill up with horned owls. Mother and Father Owl, their young, and their young's young would all line up to peer in our windows at night and watch their favorite television show: us.

Ten years after we came to live in the old house I had occasion to require the services of a lawyer. I hired the head of a prestigious law firm in Southern California, a man so powerful he was known to terrify his opponents in the courtroom and leave them speechless. Well, I saw him terrified and left speechless by my owl. And I still get the giggles when I remember that night.

It was late June and Mr. Bandit (I have changed his name to one more suiting his profession) and I were sitting out in our courtyard enjoying an after-dinner brandy. As we were talking, Father Owl swooped across the yard and flew up to the highest branch of a eucalyptus tree that overlooked our motor court.

"What was that?" my friend asked.

"A great horned owl," I answered.

"You know, Tita, I don't think I've ever really seen one," Bob Bandit mused.

"Seriously? Well, come on out on the front lawn with me, Bob, and I'll call him down so you can see one up close."

"You'll call him down?" My citified attorney could hardly keep the amusement out of his voice.

"Umm, I think so. If you'll stand just behind me out here beside this Kentia grove and stay very still, I'll see if he'll come."

Standing in front of Mr. Bandit, I sent forth a long "who-whoo-whoo-whoo" and waited. I could feel Bob's eyes on me. I knew how

I looked; like an idiot, that's how. And I prayed my owl would not be put off by a stranger. He wasn't. He took off and sailed directly toward us in a long, silent glide.

Now, a great horned owl in full swoop with his wings extended is an awesome sight to behold. They are the 747s of the owl world.

"My God, Tita! He's going to hit us," gasped my dandified friend.

"No, Bob," I murmured, "he won't do that."

The owl pulled up gracefully and landed on a palm frond close above my head.

"Now you can have a good look at him, Bob. Bob?"

I turned but my lawyer was no longer standing behind me. He was nowhere to be seen. There was a large oak at the edge of the palm grove, and as my eyes swept past it, I saw a hand holding onto the bark. There was Bob, behind the tree, his face the color of a pail of milk. He was utterly speechless. A portly man, deliberate of stride, he must have moved faster than he'd moved in years.

"I didn't think you could move that fast," I laughed, because I'm not afraid of owls or powerful attorneys.

"I didn't think I could either."

He regained his composure, took me firmly by the arm, and marched me into the courtyard. "Now, we will sit down, my dear, and while I finish my brandy, you'll tell me how you call owls out of trees."

Mr. Bandit and I won our case and have remained friends to this day. But I'll bet he's glad he doesn't have to face great horned owls in the courtroom.

In 1987 I had to sell the old house. The legal bills for that case were staggering. Our children were grown and living else-where, and nine bedrooms seemed suddenly empty, lonely. We broke off six acres from the thirty-one I owned and sold them, along with the house, to a friend and neighbor. He promised to leave the palm grove intact and to disturb the land as little as possible. We moved into a smaller home located on the remaining twenty-five acres.

A week after escrow on the old house closed, I came home one afternoon to hear the whine of chain saws and the crash of falling trees. Surprised and curious, I was walking toward my golf cart when our gardener rushed up to me, his eyes moist.

"Oh, it's terrible what they're doing," he cried. "The poor owls. The poor owls."

Racing my golf cart up my driveway, I came to the site of the massacre. Giant eucalyptus trees lay on the ground like Gulliver's Pick-up Stix. Was it the chain saw's screaming I heard, or was it the trees as one by one they were cut down?

Oh, God! It's nesting time. But the trees were no longer on my land, and I could only press my face against the cold chain link of the fence and weep.

As I was getting into the golf cart to flee that horrible scene, a great horned owl flew noiselessly to me and perched on the lowest branch of a tree to my left. An owl flying at three thirty in the afternoon? Unheard of. It was Mother Owl, and she bobbed and weaved and swayed on that branch like something possessed. She was a silent picture of anguish and confusion. As silently, the tears poured down my face and I turned to the owl.

"I'm sorry," I whispered. "I'm so sorry."

For a brief time we grieved together, and then she took off, going low over my golf cart and soaring into the sunlit sky. I never saw her again.

There was worse to come. A few days after the felling of the eucalyptus forest, one of our neighbor's workers came to find me. He was holding something in both hands, and he was clearly upset.

"I found this in the underbrush when we were cleaning up the trees," he said.

He was holding the body of a large great horned owl. It was impossible to tell if this was Father Owl, but it was possible to tell one thing: a .22-caliber bullet was lodged in the owl's chest. I know that neither the new owner nor his friends would shoot an owl or any other animal. They are gentle folk. And I thought if this was Father Owl, then his partner would not take another mate and would raise no more babies.

The palm grove went next, not to the chain saws because Kentia palms that size are worth a lot of money. They were carefully dug up and removed. Then the old house fell victim to the bulldozer. It was too old and not fancy enough, not built in the grand style. An enormous new house went up in its place.

When a wild creature gives you his friendship and trust, it is a gift of inestimable value. Father Owl had given me such a gift, a silver boon to treasure my whole life through. In selling that house I feel I betrayed my owls, but I could not have imagined what would happen once my property was no longer mine.

With their habitat destroyed and their food source gone, the great horned owls have gone. The nights are quiet now, and I am lonely for my big feathered sentinels. Rarely, rarely I do hear the call of the great horned owls as they come by to hunt. Lying in my bed, I listen to their cries and I wonder where they nest and what they eat. And a part of me cries, too.

The Heart of a Beagle

*I*f you bring one more dog into this house, I'm going to divorce you, Tita. And I mean it!"

My husband's large frame was sprawled comfortably in our green contour chair. I was standing directly in front of him, my parka half zipped as it was a winter's evening in Solvang and it was cold. Gerry was speaking in his "loud serious voice," and I knew he meant every word.

So, I was in big trouble. A beagle puppy was stuffed up under my parka, and at the sound of my husband's stentorian tones, it had begun to crawl toward the opening in my zipper. Poor thing. It probably needed a drink, or else it wanted to breathe. Either way, I figured if I was going to give my spiel, now would be a really good time.

"Gerry," I began carefully, "I didn't deliberately set out to get another dog. There was this lady in the beauty parlor and she was telling everyone she had a litter of beagle puppies for sale, and so I followed her home just to have a look. Well, this little fellow came toddling up to me, tripping over his ears and—well—he *is* AKC registered—and so—" As I was talking, the pup's nose had appeared at the opening in my jacket, followed by two bright eyes, and then his whole head was out, tripped-over ears and all.

"Oh, God!" my husband groaned as he reached for the puppy. "Give him to me. Give him to me." I plopped the small, wriggly body into Gerry's big hands and stood by contentedly while he hugged the baby dog. Sometimes, I thought, the best way is straight through. Woodstock had just joined the Lanning family.

If there is anything more appealing than a beagle puppy, I don't know what it is. This one had the added attraction of being extremely smart and with very sound instincts. One night we were sitting in our family room watching the movie *Mayerling* on television. Four-month-old Woody was sound asleep in his bed by the fireplace. One of the scenes in the movie was of a fox hunt. As the master of the hounds put his horn to his lips and blew a clarion call, Woodstock leaped from his bed, raced the length of the room, rounded the coffee table like a canine sports car, and jumped back into his bed. His eyes never opened.

"What was *that* all about?" I asked.

"Woodstock heard the call to hounds, and although hare is his game, he did what he was bred to do," replied my husband, "even sound asleep."

Lacking a plethora of rabbits in our neighborhood, Woody turned his attention to gophers, much to our delight. The first gopher was deposited on our doorstep one morning with a proud Woodstock standing over it. The dead vermin was mangled and dirty and disgusting.

"Oh, Woody! It's all mangled and dirty and disgusting," I said, and I reached for a piece of newspaper, wrapped up the gopher, and deposited it in the trash can next to our back door. I forgot to thank Woody for his gift. Undaunted by my lack of gratitude, Woodstock brought me another filthy gopher the next day. Once again I exclaimed at the revolting body, wrapped it up, and disposed of it.

A few mornings later Woody scratched at our back door. Marisa was home from school with a cold, and we both reached the door at the same time. On the doorstep stood Woody with a bulky package in his mouth. Taking it from him, Marisa showed me another dead gopher. But this one was somewhat covered up by an old piece of butcher paper that had been lying on the ground.

All the children were in school; Gerry was at work; not a soul was in our side yard. This gopher had been rather clumsily wrapped by Woodstock himself. Marisa and I leaned on each other, weak with laughter. But we did thank Woody for his present.

Because my husband was a schoolteacher, we had the summers off, and early in June we would pack up the dogs, pack up the duffle bags, and with our boat in tow, we would point the old station wagon towards British Columbia and spend the summer fishing, picking berries, and visiting our relatives on Saltspring Island.

One of our favorite pastimes was digging for clams. Woody entered into the spirit of things wholeheartedly, zeroing in on a squirting clam and, sand flying before his paws, would dig madly until he had uncovered it. This we would toss in our bucket. He became so proficient at clamming that he could even hold his breath, thrust his nose underwater, and retrieve a surface clam for our cheering children.

On our way home one summer we stopped overnight at my cousin's house in Tacoma, Washington. Strolling to their dining room that evening, our relatives walked us through their garden and pointed with pride to their rare and beautiful goldfish swimming gracefully around a shallow pond.

While we were dining inside, Woodstock got bored outside and decided to go clamming. Clams. Fish. What difference to a beagle? He was dancing with joy when we came out after dinner and he showed us his catch. There were all the prized goldfish lined up side by side on the brick terrace. Never again were we invited to visit those particular relatives with that particular beagle.

When Woodstock was five years old, we acquired a white German shepherd by virtue of the fact that our German shepherd bitch crawled under Bryan's bed and whelped. The birth was difficult, and two of the three pups didn't make it. And shortly, we lost the mother. But the big girl puppy thrived and grew, and we named her Antigone.

At the time we had the father shepherd, Creon, and Hercules, our basset hound, and Woodstock. From the beginning Woody took care of Antigone. He fussed over her like a mother, bringing her toys to play with and even sharing his bones. They roamed the fields behind our house and even swam in the Santa Ynez River two miles below us.

One winter afternoon, when Tigi was about eighteen months old, she and Woody took off to go wandering together. The dogs' dinner time was at five o'clock, and so we were not surprised to hear a scratch at the back door at five to five. But only Woodstock had come home.

We called Tigi, and then we went outside with flashlights and fanned out shouting her name. Nothing. The temperature was going to drop to thirty-two degrees that night, and we could not bear to think of that big gangly pup being out. How to find her in the hundreds of acres that surrounded us?

"Where's Tigi, Woodstock? Where is she?" we asked. But Woody had finished his meal and lay down for his nap. We decided to have our supper and hoped that Tigi would find her way home. During the meal I glanced over at our sleeping beagle and I said conversationally, "If you're so smart, Woody, and have such a good nose, why don't you go out and bring Tigi home?" The dog opened one eye, burped gently, and went back to sleep.

Midway through our dinner we heard a scratch at the door, and Gerry went down the hall. "That was only Woodstock," he said. "He wanted to go out."

At about nine o'clock we heard a sharp bark at the door. We all rushed to open it. There stood a weary and drooping beagle, and behind him, towering white against the night sky, was Tigi. She was in bad shape. Apparently, the two dogs had gone all the way to the river that afternoon, and Tigi had gotten into the nettles that grow along the riverbank.

We brought her into the kitchen. Her face was puffed up, her eyes were swollen shut, and she was wet and shivering. She even had nettles between her toes. She could barely walk.

"Oh, no, Dad. The poor dog. She can't see," said Larry. "She must have just lain down on the bank and waited for help."

We knew what to do for nettle stings, and so while the children scattered for medicine and cotton and towels, I sat in the contour chair and supervised Operation Tigi. The beagle flopped heavily under my chair and gave a forlorn little grunt.

"Oh, poor Woody!" I slid from my seat and onto the floor, where I gathered the exhausted dog into my arms. "Here you are, the hero, and you are being ignored!" While my family made a huge fuss over Tigi, I made an even bigger one over Woodstock.

In the thirteen years we shared with Woodstock he remained ever a jolly and faithful companion. He didn't accomplish any great feats of derring-do or appear in newspapers winning medals for bravery. But I will never forget that cold winter's night in Solvang when a valiant little beagle left the warmth of our kitchen and trudged four miles through the countryside with only one thought in mind: to find his injured friend and bring her home.

Swim Like an Eagle

She dropped like a stone. Plummeting past my window, she covered the distance from the fir tree to the sea in a matter of seconds; time enough for me to take in the huge mass of brown feathers, her legs held out in front, talons open, and the signature white head and tail. Lady Eagle had spotted a fish.

Jumping to my feet, I dashed out onto my deck overlooking Puget Sound. "Oh boy! I'm finally going to see an eagle in the act of catching a fish, skimming over the water, dropping down her feet, and snagging the fish from the water, just like in the movies," I thought.

But when I leaned on my railing and looked down into the sea, there sat Lady Eagle floating in the water, looking for all the world like a big, fat goose with a bald head. I couldn't believe my eyes.

Three bald eagles live beside my house, and I see them every day but I've never seen one sitting quietly in the water. My first thought was that she had been injured. She was facing toward me and regarding me calmly. Now, I talk to these eagles. I don't expect a reply (I'm not *that* far gone). I speak to them because I'm new to their territory and I want the tone of my voice to tell them that I come gently onto their land, that I respect them and their way of life. It must work because Father Eagle has flown onto a low branch just in front of my deck and kept me company while I've eaten breakfast.

I addressed Lady Eagle with utmost courtesy. "My dear, why on earth do you sit in the water looking for all the world like a big . . . uh . . . beautiful goose with a white head? I mean no offense."

Lady Eagle looked at me. I was close enough to her to see the expression in her black and yellow eyes. She seemed truly preoccupied and not a bit distressed. After many moments passed, she turned toward the sand spit that curves to the right of my property and she did something that astonished me.

Lowering her massive wings into the water, Lady Eagle pulled against the outgoing tide and, stroking from the front of her body to the tail, she began to swim toward the sand spit. Those same powerful wings that propel her through the sky became oars that moved her slowly, strongly through the water.

I watched in amazement as she made her way some sixty yards to land.

A female eagle is much larger than the male and can have a wingspan of up to ninety-two inches and a body length of forty-three inches. This eagle was all of that. She looked like a large barge swimming with simultaneous strokes of her wings. Once she gained land she hopped out of the water and onto the sand, hopping like an oversized sparrow.

"Good grief!" I thought. Now what?

Now came the seagulls. A half dozen of them swooping down and dive-bombing the eagle. She hunkered down and spread her wings around her like a great cloak. In time the seagulls tired of the game and flew onto the beach rocks to lie in wait. Lady Eagle shook herself, shook each wing separately and then hopped farther up on the sand. And that's when I saw it. Clutched firmly in her talons was an enormous silver salmon. He was not moving and I could only think that during the time she sat in the water the eagle was squeezing the life out of the fish. Clearly, he was too heavy to allow her to get airborne. As I watched she reached between her feet and tore off a chunk of fish. When she'd spat it out she took another bite, thus reducing the size of the salmon.

Unfortunatcly, my housekeeper had seen the drama from a window and she ran onto the deck yelling: "Mrs. Lanning, look at the eagle." We were much too close to the bird to allow for sudden movement or any noise. Lady Eagle was in the air in an instant. She flew toward the opposite end of our small cove carrying part of her fish. Two seagulls attacked her, coming in under her feet to grab the salmon. It fell into the water and disappeared. Lady Eagle soared high into the air, screaming her rage and frustration. Her shrill wail pierced my heart and I cried out: "Oh, no!"

The eagle circled the cove and then headed straight toward me, coming closer, growing larger, cowering the sky with her glory. She swooped up and plopped herself down on her favorite branch in my Douglas fir tree and there she sat, hunched over, the picture of dejection.

"Oh, Lady," I murmured, "I'm so sorry. I'm so sorry you lost your fish. Now what will you eat for supper?"

And do you know? That eagle looked right at me and she said: "Seagull."

About the Illustrators

Susanna Dupont Patmon grew up in Bellingham, Washington. By the age of sixteen, she had won several awards for her artwork. Two years later, Susanna sold drawings commercially for Hallmark and began working as a freelance designer.

In 1993, Susanna earned her associate of the arts degree in visual communications from the Art Institute of Seattle. She is an accomplished freelance artist who has taught art classes, illustrated greeting cards for Topline Imports, designed children's books, and provided consultation for Thomas Kinkade at the Front Street Gallery. Susanna and her husband Paul live in Poulsbo, Washington.

Harlene Schwartz is an accomplished artist who lives in Santa Barbara, California.

About the Author

Lolita "Tita" Lanning is crazy about animals, both wild and domestic. She was born in Manhattan and grew up in Chicago and Santa Barbara, where she was surrounded by pets and wildlife. By the age of six she had tamed a deer and named it Faline.

Lanning attended Westover School in Connecticut, where she graduated with honors in writing. She later graduated from Briarcliff College in New York. She attends the annual Santa Barbara Writer's Conference, and has published essays in *Santa Barbara Magazine* and the *Santa Barbara Writers Anthology*.

Three dogs graciously share their homes in Santa Barbara, California, and Bainbridge Island, Washington, with Tita, who is currently at work on her upcoming autobiography, *The Wit to Win*. She has four children and four grandchildren.